The BUFFALO BILLS

O. J. Simpson, Rushing Champion

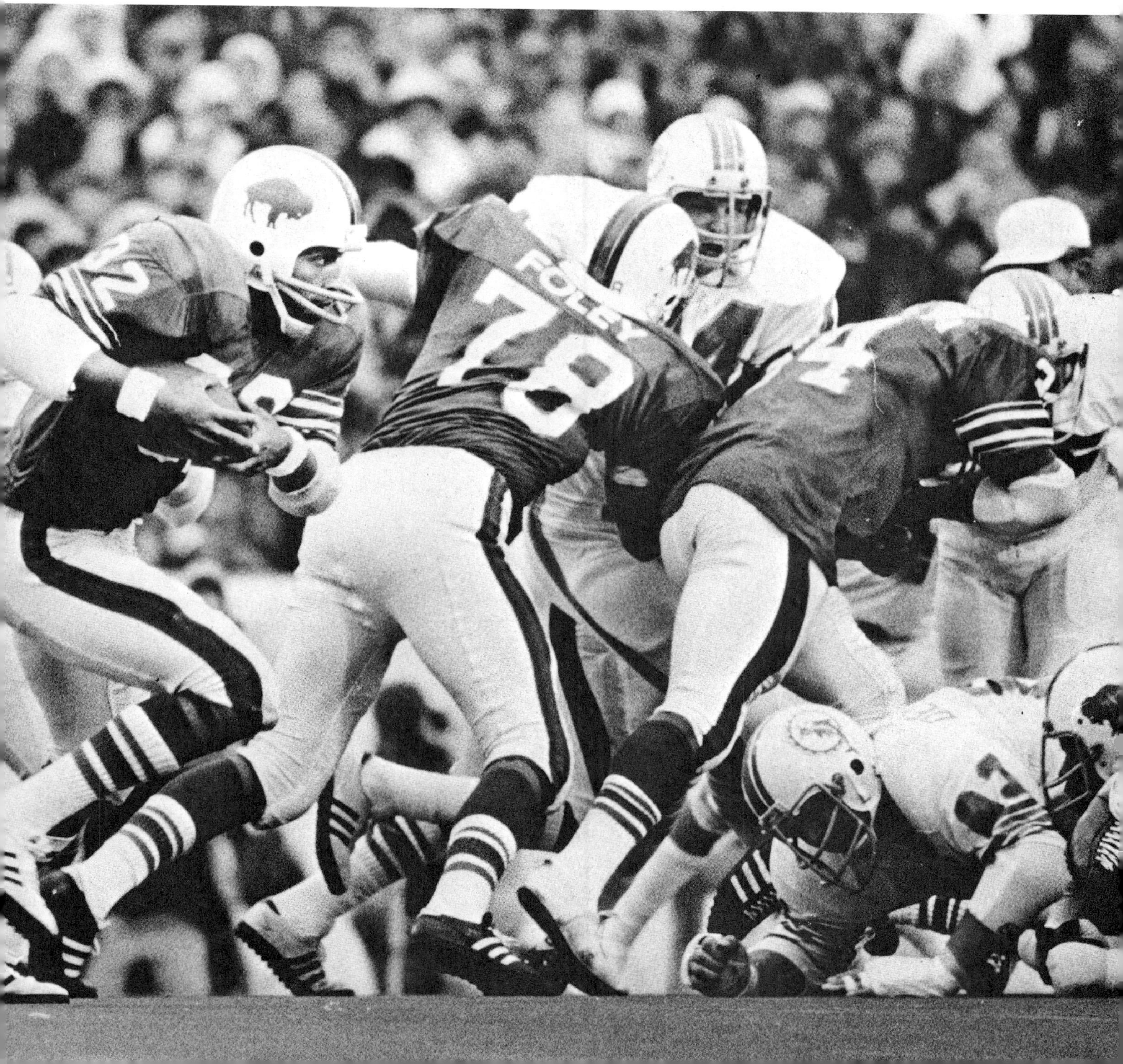

ADAMS
WATKINS
S.JONES
B.CHANDLER
KOY
MOSIER
BOGUS
ALDRIDGE

The BUFFALO BILLS

O. J. Simpson, Rushing Champion

by Jim Baker

A Stuart L. Daniels Book

PRENTICE-HALL, INC.
Englewood Cliffs, New Jersey

Art Directors: Suzanne Esper
Renate Lude
Editorial Associate: Daniel Goldschmidt
Special Projects Director: Elizabeth J. Cossa

THE BUFFALO BILLS
O. J. Simpson, Rushing Champion

by Jim Baker

Published by Prentice-Hall, Inc.
Englewood Cliffs, New Jersey

Printed in the United States of America T
Prentice-Hall International, Inc., London
Prentice-Hall of Australia, Pty. Ltd., Sydney
Prentice-Hall of Canada, Ltd., Toronto
Prentice-Hall of India Private Ltd., New Delhi
Prentice-Hall of Japan, Inc., Tokyo

Library of Congress Catalog Card Number: 74-7522

ISBN: 0-13-085803-x

Photography by:

Macolm W. Emmons
Joe Bongi, Jr.
Carl Skalak, Jr.
Robert B. Shaver
Louis Requena
Clifton Boutelle
Studio 41

o.j. and new records

Through five long and agonizing seasons, the Buffalo Bills had been gradually written off by football fans outside their home town.

They were a losing team, lacking offensive punch and defensive tenacity, groping aimlessly without a plan for the future. The one "name" player they had picked up was a fallen star. They were hopeless. Or so the reasoning went.

Suddenly, in 1972, the team began to stir. Although the losing streak continued, the star began to glow again. When the final game of the season ended, he emerged as the National Football League rushing champion.

One year later, with the 1973 campaign about to wind down, the Bills were in a different world. In one season they had been transformed from losers into winners. Now they were about to make history. On this snowswept, frigid day in New York's Shea Stadium it seemed that the whole world was watching.

O.J. Simpson—the dashing young man with No. 32 on his back, the fallen star who had picked himself back up, the College Athlete of the Decade who had suffered the indignity of being asked to his face "Whatever became of you after you left Southern Cal?"—was ready for his triumph.

The Shea Stadium scoreboard says it all but O.J. went on to break the magic 2,000 mark later in the day.

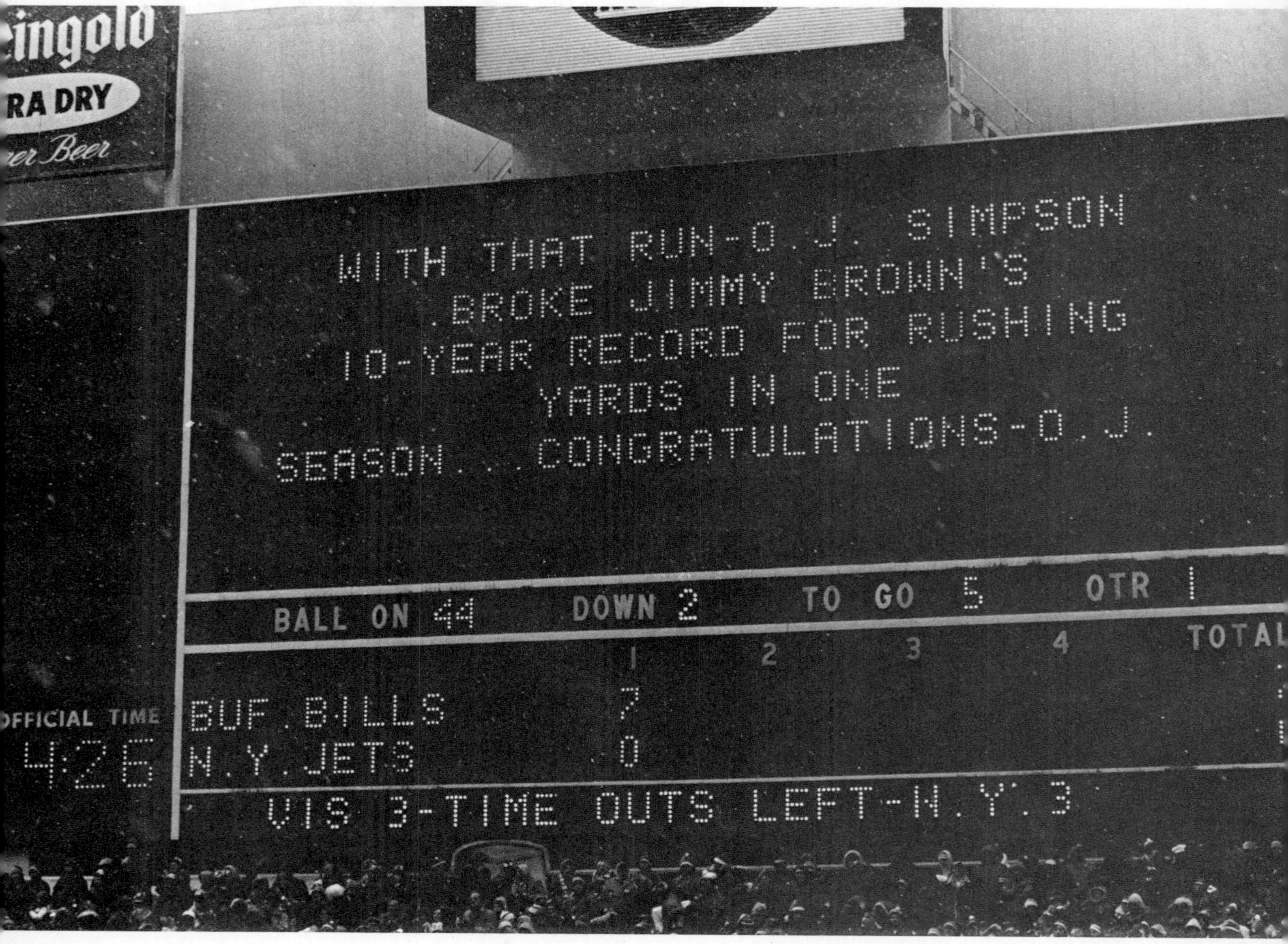

O.J. needed eight carries and 61 yards to break the single season records of former Cleveland Browns' great Jim Brown. That big fullback's 1,863 yards gained in 1963 had seemed unsurpassable until now but O.J. was close and determined.

He carried seven of the first eight plays after the opening kickoff, gaining 57 yards against the Jets, passing the 5,000-yard career mark and becoming the NFL's 20th player to claim that feat. The Bills scored and O.J. needed one more good burst to break Brown's records.

The chance came immediately after the Jets punted. Guards Reggie McKenzie and Joe DeLamielleure cleared a path, fullback Jim Braxton threw a key block, and O.J. slithered six yards. McKenzie, O.J.'s main bodyguard, raised his arms in triumph. O.J., mobbed by his teammates, lugged the football to the sideline and embraced Coach Lou Saban. The "Juice" was the No. 1 single-season rusher of all time!

He was far from through, however.

In the fourth quarter, with the Bills' 34–14 victory locked up, rookie quarterback Joe Ferguson dashed into the huddle and announced excitedly: "I've got something to fire you guys up. The Juice only needs 60 yards!"

Everyone knew in a flash that Ferguson was talking about the "impossible" dream concocted by McKenzie, offensive line coach Jim Ringo and several others in preseason camp: a 2,000-yard season for O.J.

A 22-yard power sweep brought the dream close to reality. Suddenly, just before O.J. was set to embark on his most significant run, the stadium lights were turned on. After all the seasons the Bills had spent in darkness, it was as if someone had chosen to spotlight this history-making play. O.J. took Ferguson's handoff and followed roommate McKenzie on a seven-yard trip into football immortality. His teammates mobbed the Juice again. McKenzie and Ferguson carried the king of the running backs to the sideline on their shoulders, his season's work completed with five minutes, 56 seconds to spare.

Heading for more yardage.

Reggie McKenzie uses a body block to protect quarterback Joe Ferguson. Ferguson has just released the pass.

The Buffalo Bills were a team to be reckoned with. They had catapulted from a 4–9–1 record to 9–5, an indication of the many years of promise ahead. But greater glory was wrapped up neatly in two incredible statistics: O.J. Simpson was professional football's first 2,000-yard rusher with 2,003. The Buffalo Bills were the game's first 3,000-yard rushing team, with 3,088.

In the Shea dressing quarters, O.J. needed a special room to be interviewed by a near-record press crush. Refusing to take the spotlight alone, he brought his entire offensive unit with him and introduced each player. "Gentlemen, this is Reggie McKenzie," he beamed. "He's my main man."

The awards flowed as freely as the Juice had all season. Associated Press Male Athlete of the Year, Professional Football Player of the Year by unanimous decision, winner of the Hickock Belt, Dunlop Pro Athlete of the Year; O.J. took every major football "top player" award with ease. There was simply no other player who could challenge him.

That cold afternoon in New York, December 16, 1973, O.J. had established four NFL records, bringing his season total to seven. The four league season marks set in New York were most carries (332), most rushing yards (2,003), most 100-yard games (11), and most 200-yard games (3). Indeed two of his statistics were close calls. It took a post-game check at Shea to uncover two additional yards, bringing his day's total to exactly 200. And he missed a 12th 100-yard game by only a yard, having run for 99 in a crucial 16–13 loss to Cincinnati.

O.J.'s three other records set in 1973 were most rushing yards in one game, 250 in the season opener at New England; most rushing attempts in one game, 39 against Kansas City in a smashing Monday night national television performance; and most consecutive 100-yard games over two seasons, seven. "Someone will break the records, but I'll always be the first to break 2,000," O.J. smiles.

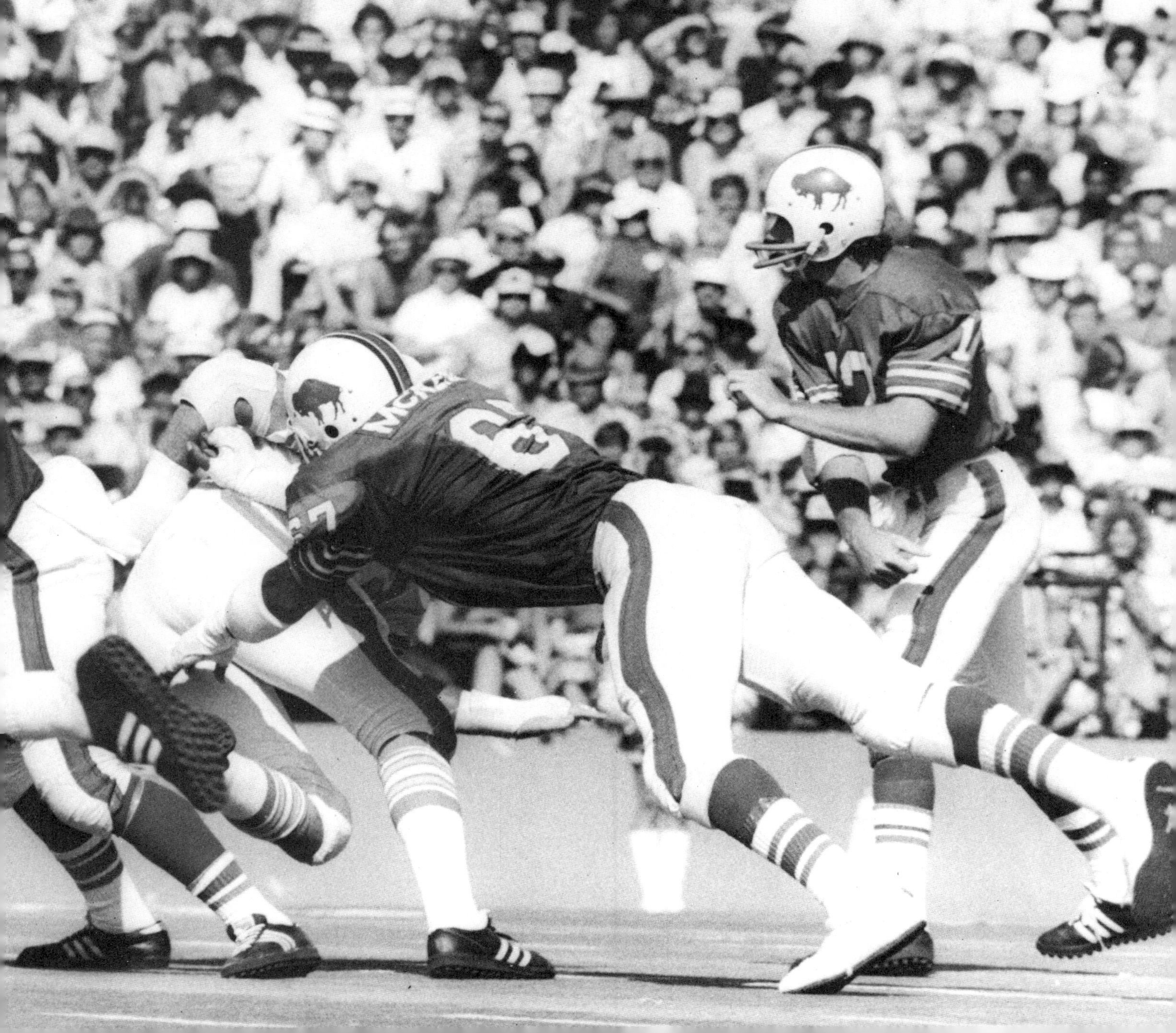

32

O.J. Simpson's unique running style affords him the opportunity to go outside on an end sweep, up the middle on a line buck, or off tackle with equal effectiveness.

Since 1972, when Lou Saban returned to the Bills for a second go-round as head coach, the Juice has nearly rewritten the club's rushing record list. Most of the previous standards were established by fullback Cookie Gilchrist and halfback Wray Carlton, stars of the Buffalo 1964 and 1965 championship teams when they were in the American Football League.

"Lou Saban saved my career," O.J. says. "He told me he'd give me the football and an offensive line and he's sure kept his word. I promised him I'd do the best I could and I think I've kept mine."

When O.J. talks about his career being saved, he is referring to the dark period, the "three lost years" he spent with the Bills after they won him in the 1969 NFL draft. He was so celebrated as the Heisman Trophy winner from USC that the race for the worst pro record in 1968, which would mean leadoff slot in draft choice, was dubbed "The O.J. Simpson Bowl." Buffalo finished the season 1–12–1 and claimed rights to the most coveted runner ever to spring from the collegiate ranks.

Lou Saban has coached three AFL teams: the Patriots, the Bills and the Broncos.

As a 1969 rookie, O.J. gained 697 rushing yards, ranking sixth among American Football Conference runners. That would be a good season for most backs, but it was far short of the super-figures expected of O.J. There was a reason: head coach Jim Rauch didn't believe in building his offense around one man and, incredibly, often used Simpson as a decoy. "We expect him to be a good pass receiver and a blocker as well," Rauch said.

O.J. was bewildered and upset. He was not being used often enough to do what he does best—run with the football. He heard the boos from the Buffalo fans in antiquated War Memorial Stadium when he stutter-stepped behind the line of scrimmage and, seeing no holes, was thrown for losses. Most disturbing of all, the pattern continued through the 1970 and 1971 seasons.

O.J.'s second season was cut to eight games when he sustained a knee injury in a crushing 43–14 loss to Cincinnati. He had started well but at the end of the year he had only 488 yards in 120 carries. Significantly, the Bills never won a game with O.J. out of the lineup.

Eagle defensive lineman Gerry Philbin i kept guessing by Buffalo's fast-steppin O.J. Simpson.

While 1970 was abbreviated for O.J., 1971 was a general disaster. Rauch, whom O.J. and other Bills called "Satan," appeared on a Buffalo TV show and criticized two popular players, Ron McDole and Paul Maguire. Club owner Ralph C. Wilson Jr. came to town, saw a taping of the show and told Rauch he publicly would defend the players. Rauch replied that if Wilson did that, he could find himself a new coach. Player personnel director Harvey Johnson was asked to take over the team.

Wilson had no other choice. NFL teams already were in preseason camp and there weren't any head coaching candidates available. Johnson, a humorous and likeable man but not a head coach, guided the Bills through a 1–13 season and O.J., with 742 yards this time, couldn't wait to catch the plane to his off-season home in California. It was no secret that he wanted to be traded. Then Lou Saban returned to Buffalo, handed Simpson the ball, and told his teammates: "There's your meal ticket. Block for him." O.J. won the 1972 league rushing title with 1,251 yards in 292 carries and the Bills, definitely looking up, upset Washington in their season finale.

That all seemed dwarfed by 1973, however.

What kind of man is Simpson? For the best illustration of his character, retreat to the Shea Stadium locker room after his triumphant 1973 finale. Having left the field early to be protected from a crush of admirers, he stood in the doorway of the Bills' room and personally shook the hand of each player as he entered after the game.

Then he gathered the entire offensive unit in with the press corps and let each member, no matter how small his contribution, share in the glory. "These are the cats who did the job all season long," O.J. said. His teammates beamed in appreciation.

The "team man" in Simpson is often obvious. "Now when Howard Cosell talks about the Bills on the Monday night game, it's about how improved we are and how we're winning, not something negative like it used to be," O.J. says. "Things like that make you feel first class."

Coach Lou Saban has a fine 51–32–4 lifetime record with the Buffalo franchise.

32
77

He has matured in his five Buffalo years. "I've settled down a lot," he says, "I hope I've grown through a lot of unpleasant experiences in the past, like being booed for the first time. Sometimes bad experiences help a person grow, become more realistic."

Now O.J. can smile about the toughness of his first three pro years, and the charge that he was "walking on eggs" then. "I didn't mind people saying I might be just another Heisman Trophy winner who didn't make it big in the pros, but what hurt was all that talk about doing the stutter-step back of the line of scrimmage," he says.

"A lot of people thought I was messing around back there. Look, no one would have liked not to have been messing around more than me. There was just nowhere to go.

"I remember how frustrating those years were," O.J. continues. "I knew I had to learn how to block and run pass patterns. But I thought I'd be running at the same time I was learning. I just wish Coach Saban had been here from the beginning. Then things wouldn't just be coming around."

O.J.'s football goal is summed up in two words: Super Bowl. He says he'll definitely play through 1975 and, if the Super Bowl appears on the horizon, he'll stretch that another year.

Even now he is not confining his activities to football. First he has a rash of commercial deals ranging from orange juice to suits. Then there is a blossoming television career with ABC's "Wide World of Sports." And then there are acting roles on TV and in the movies. In early 1974, O.J. was making "The Klansman" with Lee Marvin and Richard Burton, playing a "heavy", and reading four other scripts passed along by his business manager, Chuck Barnes of Sports Headliners, Inc.

Still, playing football, his style, is O.J.'s main concern. To do this he needs just enough blocking to let him play one-on-one with a linebacker or defensive back. These conditions usually result in major first-down yardage and often a touchdown.

When he is not running or going out for a pass, O.J. Simpson does some blocking as demonstrated here against the 49'ers veteran defensive tackle, Charlie Krueger.

RIDDELL

O.J. Simpson was the Bills' and pro football's number one draft choice in 1969.

O.J. readily admits he doesn't look for hard contact. "Guys like Larry Csonka and Larry Brown feel they should run all over people," he says. "I don't. I think I have to get as much as I can and the way to do that is run around people rather than try to go through them. I admire slashing runners. I admired Ronnie Bull when he played for the Chicago Bears. But Bull had a couple of good seasons and then all the hard knocking took its toll.

"The runners I patterned myself after were Hugh McElhenny, Willie Galimore and Gale Sayers. I think I'm the sort of runner they were."

The result? Ask Walt Michaels, the defensive coordinator of the Philadelphia Eagles, who watched the Juice squeeze 171 yards from his troops in a 27–26 Buffalo win. "It's not so much what you do wrong as what he does right," says Michaels. "You think you have him and poof, he's gone. He's just so damn dangerous."

With a football "lifetime" contract in Ralph Wilson's vault, what he really is as the Bills look toward the Super Bowl is: "The Franchise".

O.J. Simpson dodges two Jet Defenders, while following the blocking of Bruce Jarvis (51) and Dave Foley (78).

32
81
GET

Dennis Shaw releases the pass just as Dennis Wirgowski of the Patriots plunges through the offensive line.

early days

The collapse of the All-America Conference after the 1949 season had left Buffalo a city without a football franchise. It wasn't until 1959 that a Detroit insurance and trucking executive named Ralph C. Wilson Jr. gave the Queen City another major league breakthrough—a franchise in the new American Football League.

From childhood, Wilson had been an avid football fan. He wanted to own a team and made repeated efforts to acquire an NFL franchise, either through expansion or purchase of an existing team. The most he managed was to become a major stockholder in the Detroit Lions, and that only made him hungrier for a team of his own.

The AFL was created by men who had been similarly frustrated in their attempts to enter the NFL. Wilson was the seventh man to join their ranks. All he needed was the right city for his franchise and after much deliberation and consultation he decided Buffalo was it.

Earl Edwards (73) and Tony Greene pursue the elusive Mercury Morris.

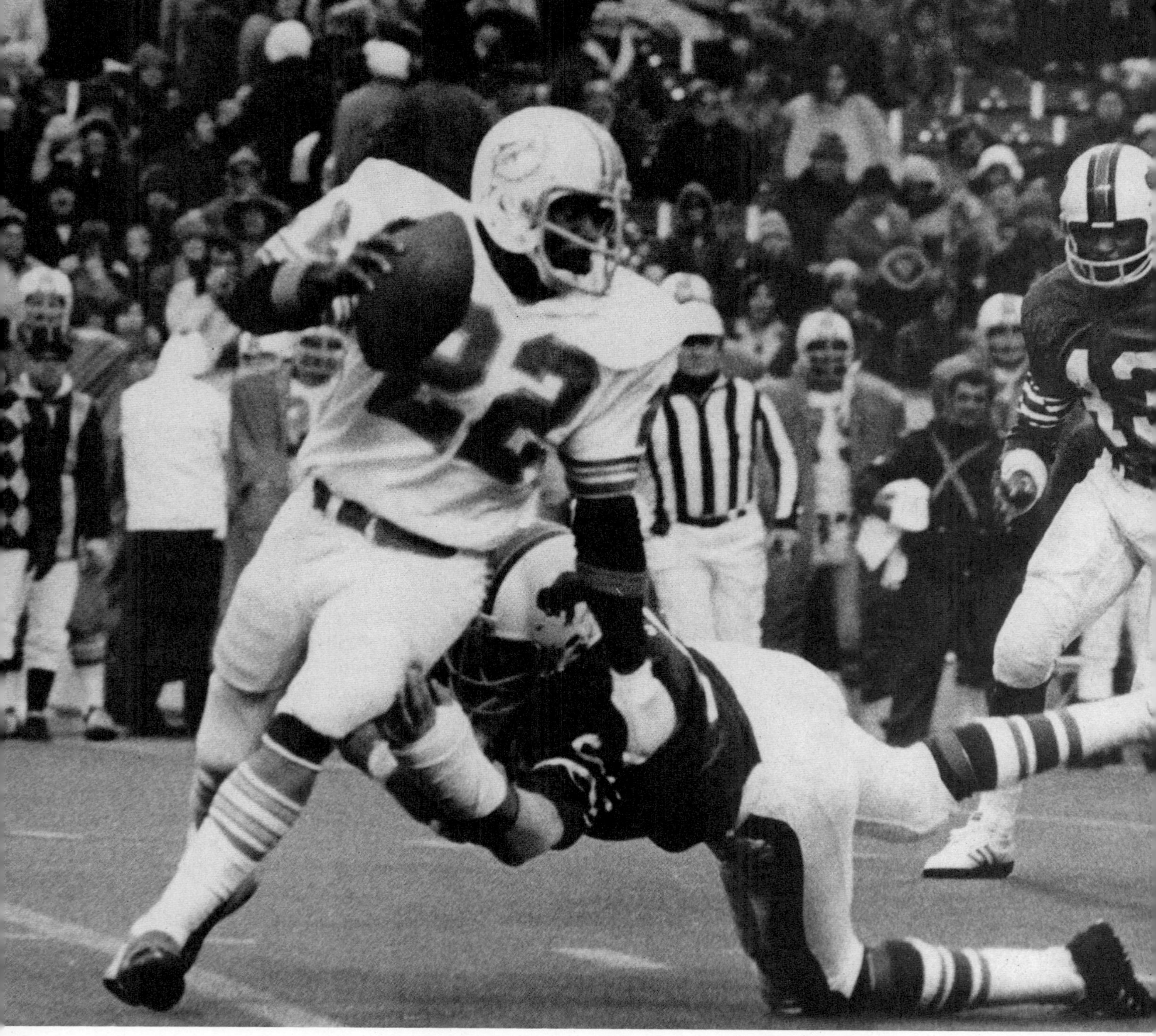

He had been convinced by some of its most prominent citizens that the city was one of the greatest sports towns in America''.

The announcement that Buffalo would enter the AFL was made on Oct. 17, 1959 and Wilson put up a $100,000 performance bond. On Nov. 20, the club signed a lease on the city's War Memorial Stadium. On Nov. 23, Penn State All-America quarterback Richie Lucas became the team's first drafted player. After fan sentiment indicated strong preference for the old team name, Wilson announced on Nov. 30 that the club would be called the Bills. The fans rejoiced. The Bills were back in town.

The pieces continued to be put together. On December 5, tackle Joe Schaffer of Tennessee became the first signed Bill. Eleven days later, Garrard (Buster) Ramsey was appointed the head coach. On December 22, Dick Gallagher became the general manager. Gallagher had been Wilson's choice as general manager long before the franchise was secured. As Paul Brown's first lieutenant in Cleveland, it was Gallagher who had signed the likes of Jimmy Brown, Bobby Mitchell, Preston Carpenter and Milt Plum.

Ramsey was well known to Wilson as the tough tutor behind the Lions' great defensive units from 1952-59, with Detroit winning three NFL titles and finishing second once during that span. A volatile type who later was to threaten to throw flanker Elbert ''Golden Wheels'' Dubenion from an airplane, Ramsey was given a three-year contract. He lasted two years.

The Bills celebrated the New Year by signing Lucas. Bob Dove and Floyd ''Breezy'' Reid were signed as assistant coaches and Harvey Johnson, a former New York Yankee and holder of the conversion kick record in the All-America conference became assistant coach and director of player personnel on May 4. He still holds the latter position.

The Bills opened their first training camp in East Aurora, New York, a Buffalo suburb, and on July 29, 1960, the day before the AFL's first exhibition (Boston vs. Buffalo at War Memorial Stadium), over 100,000 fans turned out on Main Street for the Bills' Welcome Home Parade.

The Patriots, coached by Lou Saban, spoiled that home debut, winning 28–7. On Sept. 11, the Bills opened their first regular season at the Polo Grounds in New York and Harry Wismer's Titans romped, 27–3. It was on the way back from New York that Buster Ramsey, angry at Elbert Dubenion, for mishandling passes, handoffs and kicks, considered dropping him, not only from the roster, but from the plane. Buster reconsidered and Dubenion went on to catch 42 passes for 752 yards and seven touchdowns that first year. He became the Bills' first superstar.

Crowds were not large in the AFL that first year, with Buffalo's range from an 8,876 low for Oakland to a 23,001 peak for Houston and a 111,860 seven-game total. The Bills had a disappointing first season, emerging 5-8-1.

In their second season Wilson was deeply disappointed in an 0–4 preseason mark and an opening loss and nearly fired Ramsey.

Punter Spike Jones was acquired by the Bills after the first game of the 1971 season, from Houston.

On October 10, the Patriots suddenly replaced Coach Lou Saban with assistant Mike Holovak and 17 days later, Saban was hired as Bills' director of player personnel. The rumors spread quickly—Saban would be the next head coach. Wilson denied the rumors as the team finished with a 6–8 record, and middle linebacker Archie Matsos, defensive end Laverne Torczon, defensive tackle Chuck McMurtry, and defensive back-punter Billy Atkins gained All-AFL honors. Nevertheless on January 4 the axe fell. Ramsey was out, with a year remaining on his three-year contract.

Fourteen days later, the rumors surrounding Saban became fact and he named Bob Miller, Jerry Smith, Joel Collier and John Mazur as his assistants.

Defensive end Tom Day and wide receiver Glenn Bass had joined the club in '61 as free agents and Saban added to the nucleus by gaining linebacker Mike Stratton, running back Roger Kochman, defensive tackle Tom Sestak and defensive back Ray Abruzzese in the draft's late rounds.

With a new regime and many promising players, the Bills were beginning a new era. Louis Henry Saban was about to lead them on the road to the championship.

the glory years

Dennis Shaw was one of the many outstanding quarterbacks to emerge from San Diego State and join a pro team.

Saban's first season 1962 which began with a five-game losing streak and ended with seven wins and a tie out of nine tries was the Bills' first winning season. It was also their first season with superstars Cookie Gilchrist and Jack Kemp.

Gilchrist played a year for Kitchener, Ontario en route to stardom as a two-way performer in the Canadian League with Hamilton and Toronto. But as great as he was on the field, he was a terror off it and finally Cookie wore out his Canadian Football League welcome.

Johnson rushed to Toronto and brought Cookie to Buffalo, where Saban signed him. To this day, if you ask Bills' fans of that era who "made" the team, they will answer "Cookie Gilchrist". He gave the Bills devastating power at fullback and he gave them character. Saban had numerous problems handling him, but handle him he did for three brilliant years—and traded him to Denver in 1965.

Gilchrist emerged from the season with 1,099 yards, the AFL's first 1,000-yard runner. He made the All-AFL team along with linemen Stew Barber, Billy Shaw and Harold Olson.

Randy Jackson, the Bills' fourth round draft pick in '72, runs around the Chicago defense.

The Bills were then able to obtain Jack Kemp, a first-class quarterback, from San Diego, who made his first appearance in the eleventh game of the 1962 season. Figuring in three Buffalo triumphs in the final four games of the season, he wound up in the All-Star game.

The AFL's big breakthrough in signing draft choices came after the next draft and Buffalo landed its first two "name" picks, Michigan State center Dave Behrman and Mississippi defensive tackle Jim Dunaway. But just as significant was a quarterback drafted number 24 and signed quietly before he became the MVP of the East-West Shrine Game. His name was Daryle Lamonica.

Thus began the Kemp-Lamonica years in Buffalo. Kemp was the starter and Lamonica the relief specialist, and while the fans enjoyed arguing over who was the quarterback, the two formed an excellent combination for the Bill's climb up the AFL ladder.

After four games in 1963 they were 0–3–1, and owner Wilson had to publicly reaffirm his faith in Coach Saban. But the team rebounded once again, ending the season with a 7–6–1 record which entitled them to an Eastern Division title playoff with Boston, the AFL's first playoff. Boston won, 26–8.

Gilchrist was named the AFL's most valuable player, displaying his strength in a 45–14 success over New York (newly named the Jets). The six-foot three, 251-pound fullback cracked pro football's single-game rushing record with 243 yards and five touchdowns in 36 carries.

The Bills had done well in their building program and were on the threshold of their best years. They had All-Stars in Tom Sestak, Shaw, Barber and Gilchrist and close pursuers in Dubenion and Kemp.

The 1964 season began significantly. The Bills won an opener for the first time, 34–17, over Kansas City and they didn't stop winning until they were 9–0 and the talk of the AFL.

Large crowds were coming out to see Buffalo now. Daryle Lamonica made the winning touchdown against his future teammates as the Bills capped a four-game home stand by edging Oakland, 23–20.

The bubble burst at home as Babe Parilli fired five touchdown aerials, leading Boston to a 36–28 upset before Buffalo's largest crowd, 42,308. The next day, disciplinary problems with Gilchrist came to a head and Saban shocked the football world by firing his controversial fullback. Cookie had walked off the field in the Boston game and sent Willie Ross in to replace him. Cooler heads prevailed a day later, however. Cookie apologized and Saban reinstated him. Kemp was the major go-between in the dispute.

Lamonica started his first game in Denver and the Bills romped, 30–19, setting the stage for December 20, when Buffalo gained its first Eastern Division title with a 24–14 win over Boston in Fenway Park.

The AFL title game was played in Buffalo. San Diego was favored, not because of their record (8–5–1), but because of their 1963 title game performance against Boston, a 51–10 rout, and their exceptional runner, Keith Lincoln. Stratton disposed of Lincoln early, as he was reaching for a Tobin Rote swing pass. With his arms extended, Stratton crashed into him full force, breaking his rib. The Chargers were leading at the time on a Rote touchdown toss to Dave Kocourek, but the Stratton play fired up the Bills.

Gogolak kicked a 12-yard field goal, Carlton scored from four yards, Gogolak hit from the 17 and a Kemp-Bass 51-yard pass play set up a Kemp touchdown sneak.

The Bills had reached the pinnacle of success with a 13–2 record. Saban had molded a cohesive fraternity of talent which would lead Buffalo into the title game for two more years. Kemp completed 10 of 20 passes for 188 yards and scored the clinching touchdown in the title bout. He was at the controls, calling brilliant games, as the Bills won the division and league titles. And there was Maguire, punting five times for a 46.8 yard average against the Chargers, twice sending the ball out of bounds inside the San Diego 10. It was a sad day for the Chargers, flanker Lance Alworth missing the game with a knee injury, and Rote ending a 15-year career on a losing note. But the champagne corks were popping in Buffalo.

O.J. Simpson, now a superstar in pro football, won the Heisman Trophy in his senior year at U.S.C.

Wayne Patrick and Paul Costa are head-hunters for the Baltimore ballcarriers in special team play.

Defensive tackle Jerry Patton yanks down Eagle running back Norm Bulaich.

Saban was named AFL Coach of the Year. Shaw, Barber, Sestak, Gilchrist, Stratton and Saimes made first team All-AFL. Gogolak was the AFL's No. 2 scorer with 19 field goals in 28 tries and 45 of 46 points after touchdown.

Despite all the victories, Saban had made a controversial decision. Cookie Gilchrist was going to be traded and on February 24 he was dispatched to Denver for Billy Joe, a fullback with bunion problems. The deal was not warmly received in Buffalo. Gilchrist had "made" Buffalo as surely as Joe Namath was about to "make" the AFL. Gilchrist, with 981 yards and six touchdowns as the league's top rusher, had a tremendous three-year log of 676 carries for 3,058 yards and 31 touchdowns. That three-year statistic remains a Buffalo record. For two of his three years there, he led the AFL in rushing.

The Bills opened the 1965 campaign with a 24–7 victory over Boston before a home capacity crowd. Then injuries struck, and there was no way the Bills could be as strong as in 1964. But they were still strong enough. They won their first four before being thundered at home by San Diego, 34–3. They tied the Chargers, 20–20, in San Diego, and they clinched the Eastern title with a 29–18 triumph at Houston. They wound up 10–3–1, the only winning team in the East. The AFL title clash would be with the Chargers again, this time in San Diego.

Because of that 34–3 rout in Buffalo, plus their home advantage, the Chargers were heavily favored but the Bills had never been better. San Diego couldn't get past the Bills' 24. The Bills' tremendous defense was unshakeable. Buffalo won 23–0 before a stunned Charger crowd. The Bills were AFL champions for a second season!

Kemp was named the AFL's most valuable player, an honor he richly deserved considering the direction he'd shown in the face of all those injuries! And he had a budding superstar for support in Lamonica.

Kemp, Sestak, Shaw, Stratton, Saimes, McDole, Byrd and Gogolak gained first team All-Star recognition.

Quarterback Dennis Shaw releases a pass from the pocket guarded by big Tony Greene.

The title came on December 26. The celebration was winding down when, one week later, Saban shocked the football world. Declaring that big bonuses had spoiled pro football, he announced his resignation. He said that after two titles there was little incentive left. There were rumors that he was really upset because Wilson hadn't sufficiently sweetened their arrangements, that he was tired of the handshake deals. This was denied, however, and Saban went to the University of Maryland as head coach.

Six months later, the AFL-NFL bidding war stopped when they agreed on a merger. After just one season at Maryland, Saban responded to the improved pro ball conditions by accepting a 10-year contract as head coach and general manager of the Denver Broncos. He was to serve only half that term before returning to Buffalo.

Wilson named Joe Collier, an assistant under Saban, as Lou's successor. He was immensely popular with the players, but he was not the firebrand the team needed.

There was a third straight Eastern Division title in 1966, but it was a close call. The Bills went into the AFL title game 9–4–1 and lost to Kansas City, losing, with the title, the opportunity to play in the first Super Bowl. It was a season with some triumph—they had established a new club-record scoring total and running back Bobby Burnett was Rookie of the Year. But the club was weakening, the stars were growing older, and there was not enough new talent on the horizon.

The glory years were gone.

Leo Hart just gets off the punt thanks to the blocking of Jim Braxton.

dark times – light ahead

"It was the worst trade of all time."

That was Ralph Wilson's admission several years after the 1967 trade which sent Daryle Lamonica to the Oakland Raiders for quarterback Tom Flores and wide receiver Art Powell. While Lamonica blossomed into one of the game's great quarterbacks as soon as he was given the chance to start, Flores floundered with a sore arm and Powell was well past his prime.

The trade made the Raiders a powerhouse team. This was also the beginning of a long decline for the Bills, a period that was not to end until 1973. (Even in bad years, the Bills always caused trouble for the Jets and Joe Namath who called Buffalo's stadium "The Gray Monster of the North.")

In the course of the 1967 season the Bills lost ten games, and were shut out for the first time in their eight-year history—after 142 games—23–0 at home against Boston.

Jim Braxton plunges through the snow in the 1973 season finale against the Jets.

Things got worse in 1968. Collier ordered a "punishment" scrimmage after a poor exhibition showing and during the heavy hitting Kemp sustained an injury that put him out for the season. The season opened and the Bills lost at home to Boston, 16–7. Then Lamonica and the Raiders came to town and trounced them, 48–7. Wilson could take no more. He fired Collier after the game and, with the season two weeks old and no "name" coaches available, appointed Harvey Johnson as Collier's successor.

The Bills shocked the Jets in their next game, 37–35, as Namath was intercepted five times, and three of the interceptions resulted in touchdowns for the Bills. The three interception returns for touchdowns set an AFL record for one team in one game. The record was the only highlight of the Bills' season, and the game was their only victory. Ironically, the one team the Bills could beat became the first AFL team to win the Super Bowl.

The Bills finished 1–12–1. There was one major consolation. The team with the worst record would draft O.J. Simpson. Simpson was supposed to be the player who would bring victory to the Bills again and Oakland's John Rauch was touted as the coach to lead the way. Rauch resigned from the Raiders and accepted a four-year contract with the Bills.

There was transition in Buffalo, but with Rauch and Simpson at loggerheads the won-and-lost statistics did not improve. In the changeover, two of the Bill's great stars retired. "Golden Wheels" Dubenion stepped down in October of 1968. In his nine seasons with the Bills he had gathered in 296 aerials for 5,424 yards and 36 touchdowns. All three statistics are still club records. He is also the only Bill to have caught at least one pass in 42 consecutive games. He remains the club's all-time top receiver.

Jack Kemp ended his playing days, and those as president of the AFL Players Assn., after the 1969 season. Kemp holds the Bills' passing records to this day with 1,040 completions of 2,238 passes for 15,138 yards and 97 touchdowns with 132 interceptions. His best game was a 378-yarder against Houston in 1964.

O.J. Simpson relaxes on the sidelines and talks things over with a teammate.

32

Dennis Shaw drops back to pass behind the protection of Bob Penchion.

Receiver Marlin Briscoe holds the team record for yards in a season—1036.

The Bills finished their 1969 season 4–10, and their 1970 season 3–10–1. There were some signs of promise during this bleak period. In 1970, the first season of interleague play, Dennis Shaw completed 178 of 321 passes for 2,507 yards and 10 touchdowns and was chosen the NFL's Rookie of the Year. Marlin Briscoe won the AFL receiving crown with 57 grabs. There had been another sensational come-from-behind victory over the Jets (34–31). J.D. Hill, a superb receiver from Arizona State, was the top draft choice. He joined a roster that seemed to have great potential with the likes of receiver Haven Moses, defensive end Al Cowlings and budding All-Pro cornerback Robert James, a free agent who hadn't stopped improving since his rookie days of 1969.

Before any promise could be fulfilled, Rauch and Wilson had their fight, Rauch left, and Johnson, coach in an emergency once again, led the Bills through a disastrous 1971 season in which they finished 1–13.

Then on December 23, 1971, real hope arrived in Buffalo with the return of Lou Saban. The rest, as they say, is history.

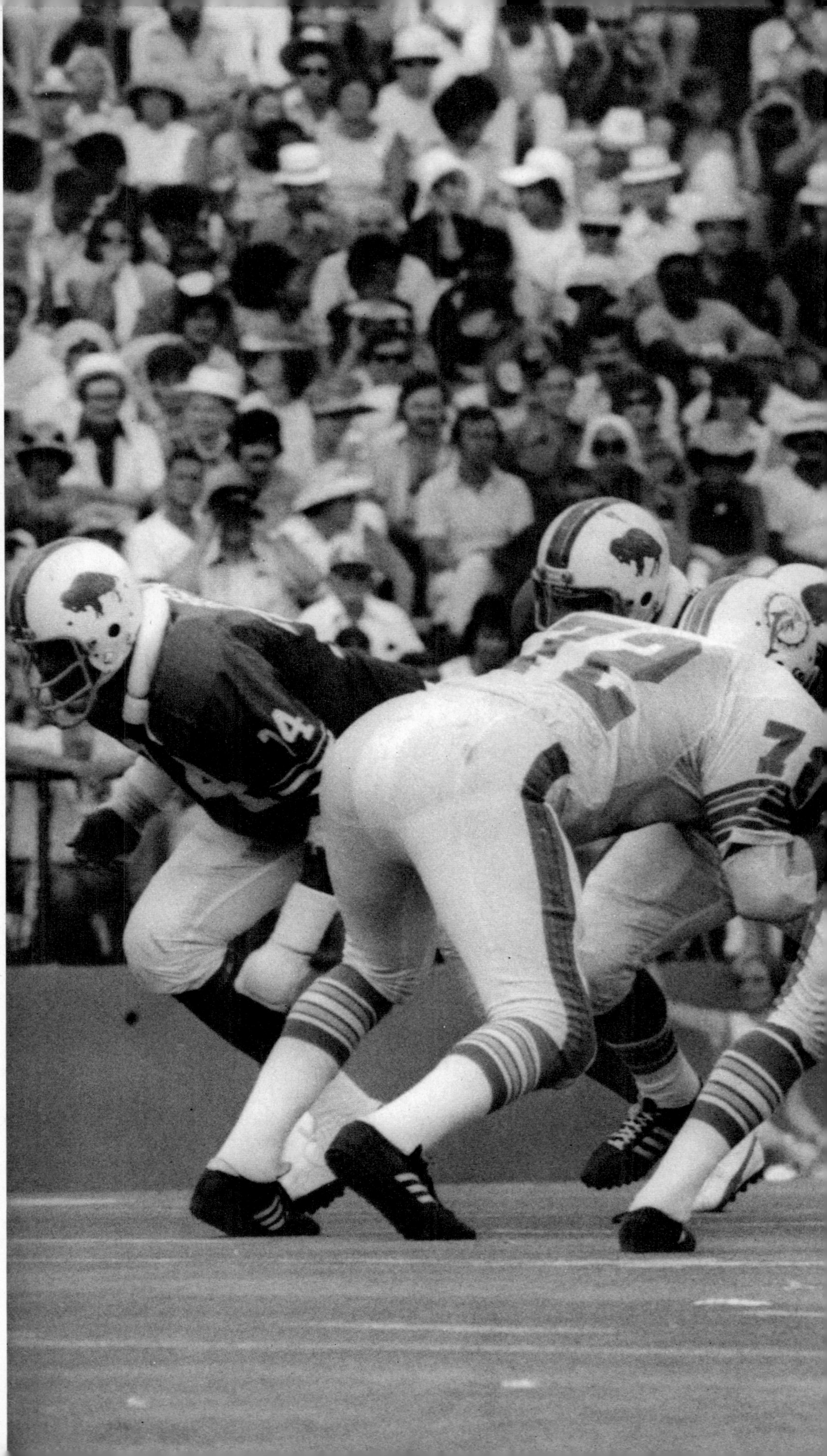

Dennis Shaw hands off as Reggie McKenzie slashes up to lead the blocking against Miami.

BILLS

the coach and his players

George Allen transformed the Washington Redskins from perennial also-rans into winners through an accent on veterans and a disdain for youth. Chuck Noll molded the Pittsburgh Steelers into contenders largely through the draft.

In Buffalo, Lou Saban doesn't frown upon veterans but he favors Noll's construction method. Along with the draft, he concentrates on trading, and makes judicious use of the waiver wire. Saban is known as "Trader Lou." He has made 35 trades and numerous waiver transactions since returning to Buffalo in late December, 1971.

Lou Saban has a deserved reputation as a master trader.

In two years, Saban steered the Bills from a 1–13 embarrassment to a 9–5 success. In 1973, the Bills registered one more victory than they had in the three previous seasons combined.

In analyzing the building job, you begin with a Saban trademark—the trenches. He constructed the AFL title teams of the mid-60's around powerhouse lines and began the same way in 1972, opening the NFL draft with Walt Patulski, All-America defensive end from Notre Dame. His number two pick was guard Reggie McKenzie, another All-American, from Michigan.

Jim Braxton, a fine runner, also performs pass blocking assignments to perfection. Here he keeps Miami linebacker Bob Matheson away from Joe Ferguson.

Running back Larry Watkins helps tight end Paul Seymour and guard Reggie McKenzie with their pass-blocking duties against the Philadelphia Eagles.

Linebacker John Skorupan heads downfield as he moves into his zone on a pass play. The pass has already been dropped by the Jets' Emerson Boozer.

Dave Foley does an outstanding job at one of the toughest spots in the NFL—left tackle on O.J. Simpson's blocking line.

The reasons were obvious. The hapless Bills of 1971, losing their first 10 games and beating only New England all year, were generally run over by their conquerors. Thus, the imperative need for a Patulski. O.J. Simpson needed blocking power and McKenzie, who had led the interference for Michigan's vaunted rushing game, was the choice.

Just before the season opened, Saban obtained tackle Dave Foley on waivers from the New York Jets. Two promising young defensive tackles were imported by the same method—Don Croft from Baltimore and Jerry Patton from Minnesota. All three were starters within a week's time.

Still, the Bills had major line difficulties through '72. Most were caused by injuries, especially on offense, with seven guards, four centers and four tackles starting at one time or another. McKenzie was supposed to be brought along slowly. Instead, he wound up the bulwark of the offensive front.

Saban knew he had to concentrate on the lines again in the 1973 draft and used his first three choices to fortify them. Paul Seymour came from Michigan as a tackle (he wound up at tight end). Joe DeLamielleure, All-America guard from Michigan State, was another first-round choice, to plug a guard hole. Jeff Winans, defensive tackle from USC, was a second-round pick.

In a large sense, O.J.'s supporting cast in 1973 was "made" through the draft. It was a highly successful operation with 10 of the 21 choices making the final roster. After Seymour, DeLamielleure (popularly called Joe D) and Winans, Saban selected Joe Ferguson from Arkansas in the third round, to replace veteran Dennis Shaw as starting quarterback.

Bob Kampa, another defensive lineman from California, was the second third-round pick. Then came defensive back Donnie Walker. He became an important safety and kick returner. Wallace Francis was next. He had been scouted by former Bills' star wide receiver Elbert Dubenion at Arkansas AM&N and he became the NFL's top kickoff return specialist, with two long touchdown jaunts, one measuring 101 yards. John Skorupan, a standout linebacker from talent-rich Penn State, was the sixth-round choice and he moved right in at strongside linebacker. Even 14th-round choice Merv Krakau

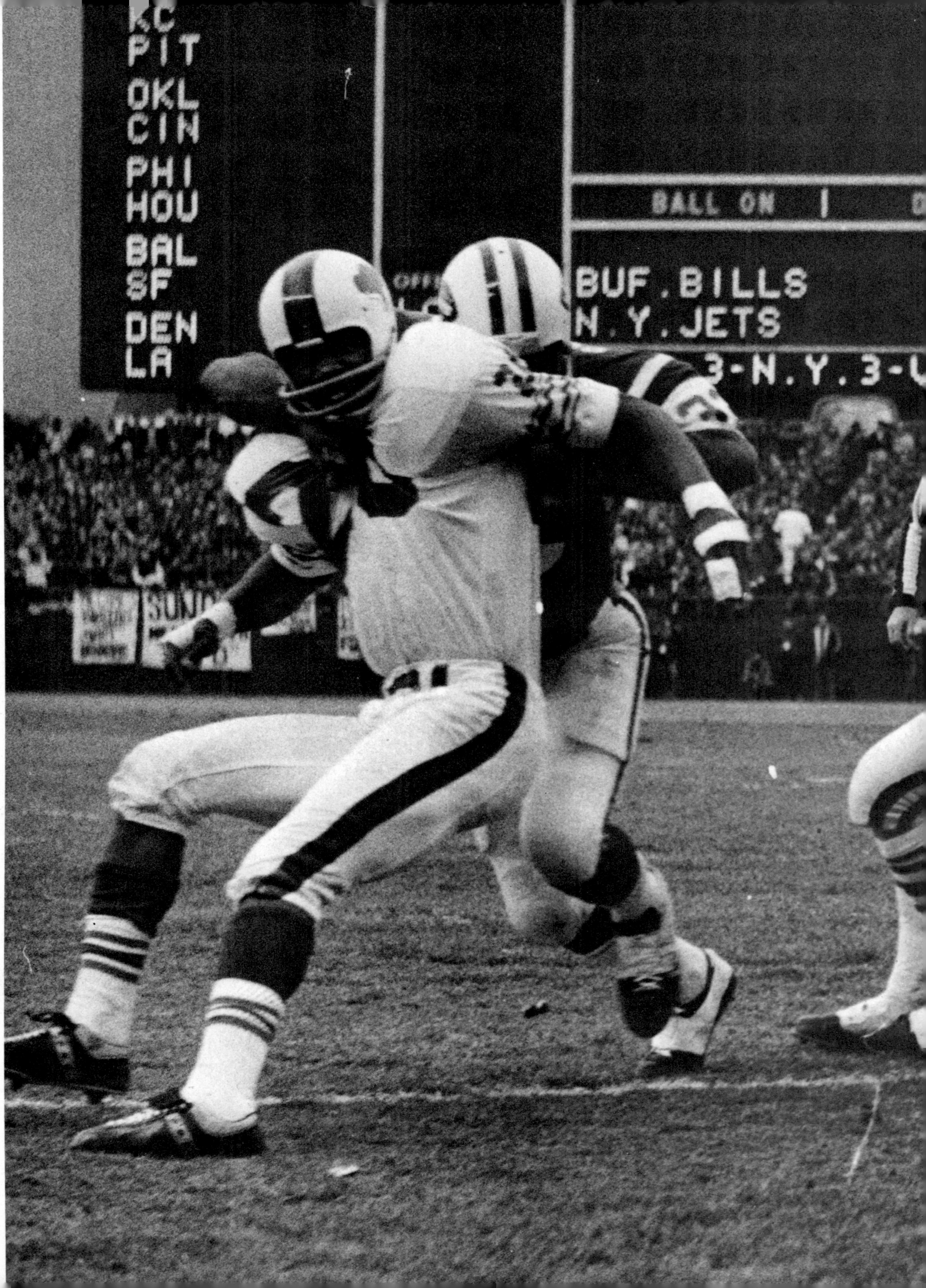

KC
PIT
OKL
CIN
PHI
HOU
BAL
SF
DEN
LA
BALL ON
BUF. BILLS
N.Y. JETS

Cornerback Leon Garror has his arm around Jet running back John Riggins in a 1972 game at the Big Shea.

from Iowa State, another linebacker, made the squad. He was the starting middle linebacker in the season opener.

What Saban couldn't manage through the draft, he went after in trade. A six-player swap with New England brought in Jim Cheyunski, former Syracuse University star and a five-year middle linebacker veteran, Halvor Hagen, who would temporarily bench Patulski and start five games at defensive end; and Mike Montler, former Colorado All-American who had four years behind him at guard and tackle. Montler wound up the starting center for the last six games after Bruce Jarvis was injured in practice.

Most experts considered the Patriot trade a Buffalo steal. The Patriots received middle linebacker Edgar Chandler, fullback Wayne Patrick (who was out injured all season) and linebacker Jeff Lyman (who was waived).

With the Philadelphia Eagles, Saban swapped Dick Cunningham, the oft-injured middle linebacker, for fullback Larry Watkins. Watkins replaced the injured Jim Braxton in the Bills' lineup and proved an excellent running mate for O.J.

The Bills' pivotal '73 trade was negotiated with San Francisco. The defensive line still needed maturity and a leader. The 49ers provided that in four-year NFL veteran Earl Edwards, whom Saban switched from tackle to end with great success. In return, the 49ers received promising running back Randy Jackson, who was injured shortly thereafter, and a 1975 third-round draft choice.

Saban's most risky deal, on the surface, sent veteran guard-center Irv Goode to Miami for defensive tackle Mike Kadish. Kadish, a linemate of Patulski at Notre Dame, had been the Dolphin's top draft pick in 1972 but had ended up with the cab squad for what Coach Don Shula considered an overweight condition. Saban was not worried about Kadish's weight and he had confidence that Joe D could do the job at right guard, making Goode expendable.

Finally, the trench positions were stocked. Patulski, Patton, Kadish and Edwards formed the late-season starting defensive wall. Kampa and Winans provided staunch support as did Hagen, who was switched to offensive tackle after five games as a defensive end

Mike Kadish (71) meets the Cincinnati lineman head-on.

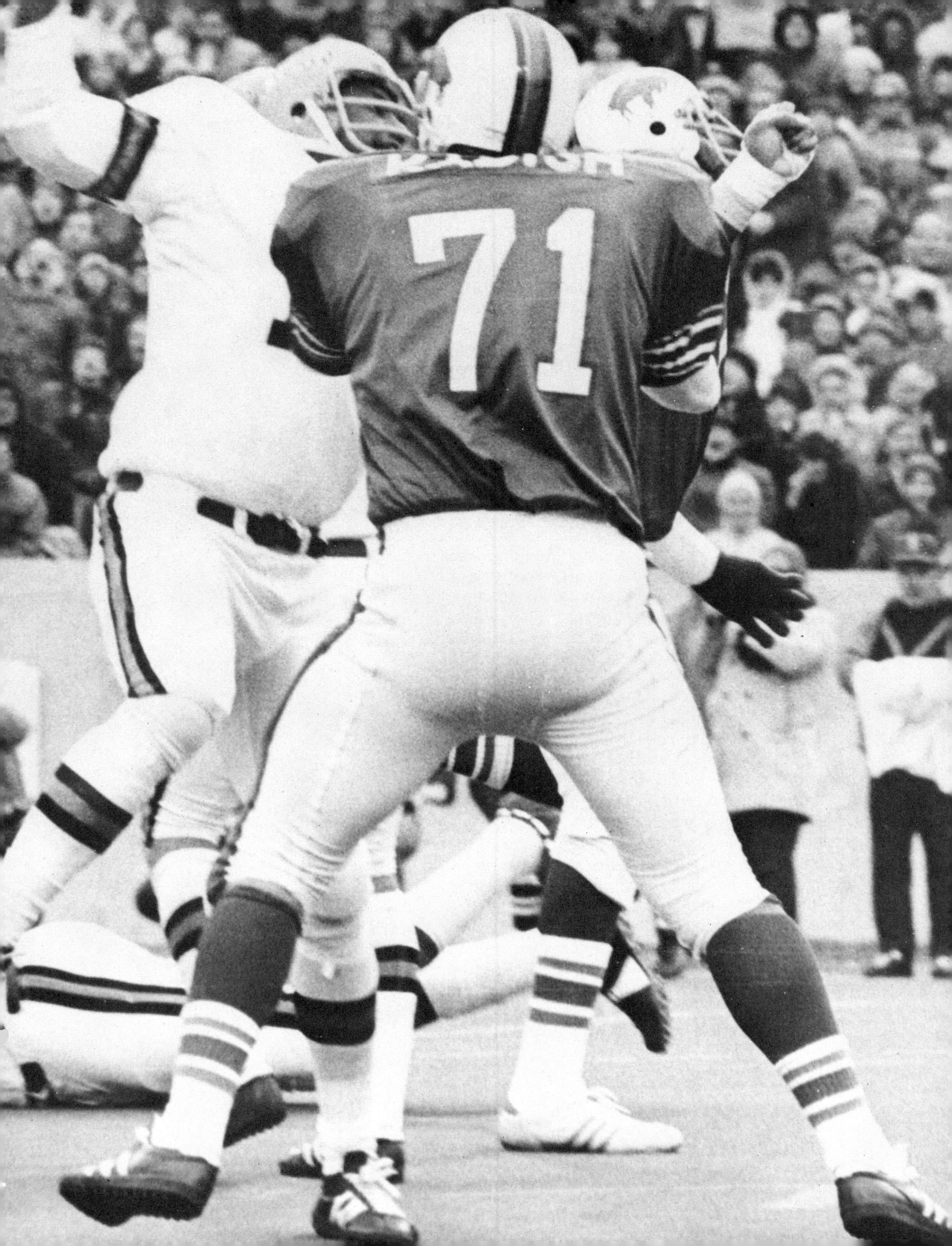
71

starter. Croft was out with a knee injury all season and Jeff Yeates, a rookie from Boston College, recently recovered from knee surgery, provided still more long-range depth.

Where injury prevailed in 1972, depth was the keynote in the 1973 offensive line. Only Jarvis incurred an injury that put him out of play for the season, and the versatile Montler was very ready to step in. McKenzie and Joe D formed an excellent guard combination and Foley remained steady with big Donnie Green at tackle. Seymour, drafted as a tackle, provided bonus blocking at tight end when veteran Jan White suddenly retired.

Saban made several other transactions for valuable roster depth. In swaps for draft choices, running back Bo Cornell was imported from Cleveland, wide receiver Ray Jarvis came from Atlanta and special teams center Willie Parker arrived from the Rams. With Parker around, there were no mismanaged snaps for punts and field goals, as there had been in '72.

There were also emergency deals, centering on the still shaky defensive backfield. After veteran strong safety John Pitts was dealt to Denver for linebacker Fred Forsberg, rookie Donnie Walker incurred a two-week leg injury and Saban lured veteran Ernie Kellerman from retirement to fill the void. Kellerman, a former standout with the Browns, was steady at strong safety the rest of the season.

Kellerman arrived in mid-week and started that Sunday. So did rookie Ken Stone, who was unemployed after being cut loose by Washington. He arrived at Rich Stadium on Wednesday and started immediately at free safety. Ironically, he wound up the season back with rookie-shy George Allen in Washington.

Dwight Harrison, whom Saban had obtained from Denver for Haven Moses in 1972, was converted from wide receiver to cornerback after a loss in San Diego. Only All-Pro corner Robert James was a sure bet in that defensive backfield for the Bills' first regular season junket at home. They won all three games.

Safety Ernie Kellerman leaps high in vain as Miami tight end Jim Mandich latches on to the pass.

Cornerback Robert James, a Buffalo veteran, tackles a Jet receiver.

Bo Cornell, who was acquired from the Cleveland Browns, runs upfield on a kick return as Miami's Curtis Johnson stumbles to the ground behind him.

Receiver J.D. Hill is upended by a Cincinnati defender after jumping high for the ball.

Despite his own outstanding running ability Larry Watkins is often called upon to block for teammate O.J. Simpson. Here he heads off Eagle linebacker Steve Zabel as Reggie McKenzie and Bob Chandler fire out on their men.

Sometimes, the house cleaning was painful. Mike Stratton, a hard-hitting outside linebacker who had spent 11 seasons in a Buffalo uniform, was sent to San Diego in another draft choice deal. He was the last of the Bills from the AFL title years of the mid-60's.

When Saban's dealing was done, the club "graybeards" were O.J. and James, both with the Bills since 1969. The roster had undergone major surgery, but the lines now were effective and deep, O.J. had blocking support and two power backs in Braxton and Watkins, the linebacking was steadier, and with Ferguson, the quarterbacking was consistent.

Ferguson had been a risky choice for the Bills. "He had a disappointing senior season," Saban said in an understatement, "but we picked him off his junior season and we think he has a fine future." After an eye-popping fireball display his first day in preseason camp at Niagara University, it was a glowing Saban who remarked, "We knew he could throw."

It was a question then of confidence, and molding a rookie to fit the long range plans of a team with a superstar running back and effective receivers like J.D. Hill and Bobby Chandler.

The receivers got their own special treatment once Saban arrived on the Buffalo scene. With an O.J. on the roster, Saban wanted everyone up front to block. Even a light speed merchant like J.D. was issued a protective cage for his helmet, and soon he was better known for his crackback blocking exploits, springing O.J., than for hauling in passes.

The 1974 draft, nationally, was talent-thin compared to 1973, but the Bills still came up with fortifying choices. Reuben Gant, impressive tight end from Oklahoma State, was the number one pick and, in time, he should move Seymour back inside. Doug Allen, an All-East linebacker from Penn State, may give the team another Skorupan. Gary Marangi, the Boston College quarterback who said no to the World Football League, joins Ferguson to make up the NFL's youngest signal-barking combination. East Carolina's Carlestar Crumpler provides further running back depth. The receiver corps was bolstered by trade as Ahmad Rashad (formerly Bobby Moore) came from St. Louis for quarterback Dennis Shaw.

The Bill defense causes a Cincinnati fumble and tackle Mike Kadish (71) lunges for the loose ball.

85
71

81

In less than three years, a remarkably short time for such an effective face-lifting, Lou Saban's Buffalo Bills became the team of his choice. Because of his shuffling, which caused one player to describe the Rich Stadium scene as "a railroad depot," it is one of footballs youngest teams.

The players he kept were of All-Pro caliber, like O.J. and James, or contenders like placekicker John Leypoldt. He has won the respect of his players, something not all Bills' coaches could claim. "He treats us like men. Everything is out in the open. That's the way I like it," says O.J.

The Super Bowl is the only major target O.J. has left. Defensively, the question marks are the backs, except for James, a proven All-Star. Offensively, the quarterback is the pivot and O.J., optimistic that Ferguson can do the job, tells how Saban has developed him carefully.

"We lost in New Orleans because we used the run all day long," he says. "We won in Baltimore and Atlanta with Joe throwing the ball. He was coming into his own toward the end of the season. We had to keep the reins on him early in the year, but he started to throw well. We can run and beat anyone if we can play them straight up—that is running and passing."

With Saban calling the signals and keeping Ferguson's pass attempts down to about 10 per game, the quarterback's statistics were last in the league. But he didn't take the physical punishment and mental anguish that Bert Jones suffered in Baltimore, either.

Ferguson recognizes the value of the way he is being developed. "If we had tried to throw all the time at first, it would have been awfully tough for me to make it," he says. "But O.J.'s running took so much of the pressure off me. I can't describe how much of a help he was."

Bob Chandler (81) holds for placekicker John Leypoldt.

There were lost games, to New Orleans and Cincinnati for instance, when it seemed that a Buffalo aerial attack would have turned things around. Yet, the weapon was hardly tried. Saban was determined to bring his prize quarterback along slowly. He had been through too many seasons with weakness at the game's pivotal slot.

To recap the highlights of Saban's pro coaching career would be close to retelling the Bills' mid-60's and 1973 success stories. He was at the helm in both periods.

As a player, quarterback was Saban's first position, earning him MVP honors at Indiana in 1942. After World War II and duty in the China-Burma theater, he starred from 1946-49 as a linebacker with the Cleveland Browns in the All-America Conference, where many of his games were against the original Buffalo Bills. Saban captained the Browns to league titles for four years and was named All-Pro in 1948 and 1949. Then the AAC folded and Saban launched the coaching career that had always been his goal.

He coached Case Institute from 1950-52 then put in a three-year stint at Washington U. as an assistant and one more at Northwestern in the same capacity. He coached Northwestern in a winless '55 campaign, then went on to three successful years at the Western Illinois helm, his 1959 team going 9–0.

He moved into the pro field with the advent of the American Football League, becoming the Boston Patriot's first coach in 1960. He moved on to the Bills as director of player personnel after five games in 1961 and succeeded Buster Ramsey as head coach the next year. It was under his guidance that the Bills won the 1964 and 1965 titles and he was named AFL Coach of the Year in 1964.

College football and the University of Maryland suddenly seemed attractive to him in 1966, but a year later he began a five-year stint as general manager and the head coach of the Denver Broncos. A winning record eluded him in the "Mile High" climate and he returned to Buffalo for another rebuilding challenge in late December, 1971. He signed a 10-year contract.

The Bills' two-year turnabout from 1–13 to 9–5, makes it clear this trip is paying off. Championship "lightning" may strike for a second time in Buffalo with Louis Henry Saban.

Lou Saban hopes to lead the Bills to a championship as he did in 1964 and 1965.

Joe Ferguson was the Bills' third round selection in the 1973 draft.

Larry Watkins (38) runs between heavy traffic against New York.

a winning season

Take one doormat football team which has won 13 games, lost 54 and tied three over a five-year span, throw in a winless preseason (0–6) and you have another ho-hum loser, right?

Surprise!

That was the Buffalo Bills' position in the fall of 1973 when O.J. Simpson took matters into his own hands and brought fullback Larry Watkins with him on a season-opening rushing spree in Foxboro, Mass. In less than three hours the Bills' image in the National Football League was drastically altered. O.J. and the former Eagles' power back had combined for 355 yards in a 31–13 conquest of the Patriots.

It was a symbolic beginning for the Bills as O.J. started his year of records with an incredible 250-yard output in 29 carries with two touchdowns. The feat cracked by three yards the NFL mark set Dec. 5, 1971 by the Los Angeles Rams' Willie Ellison against New Orleans. Watkins, also bulling for two scores, was overwhelming up the middle while O.J., with guard Reggie McKenzie pulling out to block, repeatedly ran the power sweep right—at one point attempting it on seven straight plays. The result was devastation and a Bills' two man single-game rushing mark.

The Bill defense led by Bill Cahill (22) put the stop on a New England runner.

Cornerback Donnie Walker (26) turns c
the speed after making an interception.

Chuck Fairbanks, making his New England coaching debut with that game, alluded to O.J. as "Grant going through Richmond" and Edgar Chandler, the Patriots' middle linebacker whom Saban had traded to Fairbanks in the off-season, quipped that the Juice "had more yardage than Secretariat". The Bills amassed 360 by land, another club record.

When O.J. entered the dressing room, his teammates gave him a rare tribute, a standing ovation. When he spoke, he talked of the team. "I'm glad the record came when it did," he said. "This is our first opening-day win since I've been in Buffalo and it really feels good. We can take it from here and have an outstanding season."

Still, the Bills backslid the following Sunday in San Diego. Linebacker Mike Stratton enjoyed a big day against his team of 11 years, intercepting two passes while Johnny Unitas fired for two scores in a 34–7 Charger romp.

Saban juggled his entire defensive backfield, with the exception of Robert James at left corner, after the San Diego rout. Rookie Ken Stone was imported from Washington and started at free safety. Rookie Don Walker replaced veteran John Pitts on the strong side and Dwight Harrison, who started the season as a wide receiver, took over Tony Greene's position as starting right cornerback.

What followed was a sensational three-victory home stand. Picture that makeshift defensive backfield and a Buffalo shutout in the game against the Jets until two seconds remained, when quarterback Al Woodall hit Jerome Barkum with a desperate 34-yard TD bomb while being decked by Earl Edwards.

The Bills prevailed, 9–7, in an upset authored by three John Leypoldt field goals as O.J. carried 24 times for 123 yards.

The next victim was Philadelphia. Although Walker was hurt in practice and Saban had to go with Ted Koy —a versatile sort but not a defensive back—at strong safety, and although Eagle Roman Gabriel was firing to a sensational rookie tight end named Charley Young, the Bills somehow prevailed. The score was 27–26, as Tom Dempsey's 26-yard field goal attempt sailed inches wide on the final play. O.J. had 171 yards in 27 carries.

Although Joe Ferguson has a fine throwing arm, his primary function in his 1973 rookie season was handing off to the runners who produced Buffalo's record-breaking ground game.

Buffalo had won again on Leypoldt's toe, and they had won despite the figures. The Eagles gained 451 yards to the Bills' 276 and tried 74 plays to Buffalo's 47. How did the Bills do it? "The Good Lord was with us," concluded James, the team chaplain.

The Bills capped the perfect home stand by ripping Baltimore, 31–13. The victory was highlighted by a 78-yard Simpson touchdown in which he tried an off-tackle run, then started to go wide, was cut off, reversed his field and lunged. "I was hoping to get one yard for a first down," he said. "Then I realized I could get more. I decked one of their backs and suddenly I was into the clear."

O.J. smashed the NFL record for most consecutive 100-yard games over two seasons that day, realizing his seventh straight with 166 yards in 22 trips.

Buffalo now was 4–1 and tied with the Super Bowl champs for the AFC Eastern lead. It seemed too good to last, and it didn't. The Bills next game was at Miami, where they could not manage a first-half first down. O.J. could make only 55 yards and Miami breezed 27–6.

The mark of a good team is the ability to bounce back, however, and the Bills accomplished that on their Monday night national television debut against favored Kansas City. Middle linebacker Jim Cheyunski, despite a nagging knee injury which plagued him most of the season, pounced on a fumble and intercepted a pass in the opening minutes, setting up two Simpson touchdowns and giving the Bills a 14–0 cushion.

The sellout crowd at Buffalo's Rich Stadium celebrated wildly and even Howard Cosell applauded in his booth as O.J. became the first NFL player to eclipse the 1,000 yard mark in half season. He cracked the NFL's rushing attempts mark with 39 and gained 157 yards for a half-year of 1,025. The Bills won 23–14, and were 5–2 at mid-season. Buffalo had more than a new stadium, it had a new kind of team.

Then came an airplane scare in which the Bills' charter to New Orleans lost all its hydraulic fuel and made an emergency landing in Cleveland. "We scored one victory on this trip already," said Saban when the plane touched down.

Tight end Ted Koy chases the ballcarrier in a special team's play.

GET

Wide receiver Bob Chandler is pulled down from behind after a reception by the Jets' Richard Neal.

Defensive tackle Steve Okoniewski played in the Coaches All-American and College All-Star games while at Montana before turning pro and coming to Buffalo.

It was to be their only success this trip south as the Saints, who had shocked Washington the previous week, made the Bills their first shutout victims ever, 13–0. Making up for an early-season losing streak, they challenged Buffalo with seven and eight-man fronts, daring rookie quarterback Joe Ferguson to throw. Saban wouldn't let him and O.J. ran into stacked defenses all day.

The following Sunday at Rich Stadium was better, but not good enough, as O.J. fell a yard shy of another 100-yard game and Cincinnati won, 16–13, on Horst Muhlmann's game-ending 33-yard field goal. It was the playoff crusher for the Bills.

The return game with Miami followed and the Bills' frustration mounted. The Dolphins had prided themselves in not allowing one 100-yard rusher in 45 games. The Bills mustered two—O.J. with 120 yards and the bulling Jim Braxton (having recovered from a congenital back injury which cost him a half-season) with 119 tough ones. The Bills had a 313–277 yardage advantage, two big producers, yet four major attempts fizzled and they could not score. Miami won, 17–0.

Now the Bills were back at .500 ball and a collapse seemed possible. It looked likely until late in the next game at Baltimore with the lowly Colts ahead, 17–0. But luck was working for the Bills as Baltimore center Fred Hoaglin hiked the ball over punter David Lee's head and Lee managed only a desperate short kick with Patulski hanging onto him.

Suddenly, Ferguson was allowed to throw and he displayed the brilliance of his camp days at Niagara University. He unleashed a perfect 37-yard touchdown strike to Bob Chandler and the Bills drew even with 1:34 remaining. Then luck went the Bills' way again. Colt quarterback Marty Domres spotted Dwight Harrison out of position and tried to hit his wide-open target. But he failed to notice the cornerback recovering as he cocked his arm. Harrison raced over to intercept and ran 31 yards for the winning touchdown. The Bills didn't lose another game that season. They didn't even come close to losing.

Jim Cheyunski (50), Robert James (20) and Ernie Kellerman (24) combine to stop the Dolphin ballcarrier.

The Atlanta Falcons, figuring they had a playoff berth "made" with three home games left against supposedly inferior foes, hosted the Bills the following Sunday and received a 17–6 jolt from which they couldn't recover. The Falcons are a physically punishing team, but both lines were physically whipped that day. O.J., having been "knocked" by Atlanta Coach Norm Van Brocklin for "not putting his nose in there," responded with a 137-yard afternoon. Braxton crashed over for both touchdowns and Leypoldt kicked a 20-yard field goal.

The next week, in the Rich Stadium snow, McKenzie led another power sweep against New England, and the Bills won 37–13. Ferguson was growing looser. He fired two touchdown aerials to Chandler, who was becoming his favorite target. O.J. rushed for a spectacular 219 yards.

The 219-yard statistic is even more remarkable in light of the fact that O.J. carried the ball only twice in the first quarter. Thanks to a 90-yard touchdown kickoff return by rookie Wallace Francis, who led the league in that department, O.J. did not step onto the field until almost seven minutes elapsed. Once he did, however, the Patriots didn't have a chance.

In one play he ran the power sweep and broke free from Ralph Anderson for 71 yards to the New England nine. Later, he dashed through the snow for 28 and 24 yards. When he returned to the Bills' bench after his last run, as has been stated, he was just 61 yards and 8 carries short of breaking Jim Brown's single-season rushing yardage and attempts records.

O.J. had wanted to break both records in Buffalo. "These fans have been just great to us all year and I wanted to do something special for them in our last home game," he said. But to gain 61 more yards would have been a near-impossible feat.

The Bills had far-fetched visions of a playoff berth, too, but it wasn't to be. They needed help from two other teams and, though they did their part by crunching the Jets 34–14, they were eliminated when Cincinnati edged Houston. They had to be satisfied with their record-breaking season-closer in New York, and the promise of seasons to come.

28
56

5
85
67

Headhunter Reggie McKenzie seeks out his next victim. Eagle linebacker Marlin McKeever appears a likely choice.

Pete Van Valkenberg runs behind the blocking of Ray Jarvis who faces off against Doug Swift of Miami.

MONT

Jim Braxton lowers his head and prepares to hurl himself over Atlanta defender middle linebacker Tommy Nobis.

The Bills were 9–5, finishing with a tremendous four-game victory run, and O.J. had catapulted them into the record book as pro football's first 3,000-yard rushing team—erasing the record Miami had established just one season earlier.

"All week long I was worried about 61 yards and I ended up with 2,003," O.J. told a near-record New York press crush. "When I saw the snow, I felt bad," he went on. "But then I remembered it snowed last week in Buffalo and it turned out okay."

O.J. credited Braxton, who had had a two-touchdown day himself, with the big block on his six-yard trip past Brown's record. "I landed on Jim's back and he turned over and asked me: 'Was the hole big enough?' I looked around and saw everyone jumping up and down. I smiled and said to him, 'It seems alright, I guess.' "

"After that there was no way they were going to stop us from getting 2,000 for the Juice," said McKenzie, the blockers' spokesman. "They kept phoning down from the press box so we knew how much we needed."

O.J. responded: "Maybe it's my record, but I had a lot of help. These guys were just fantastic. They kept blasting holes open and all I had to do was follow them through. That record was a team effort. No running back can get 2,000 yards without a lot of help."

O.J. expects his record to be broken someday, but just hopes it lasts a decade as Brown's did. Unless, of course, he breaks it himself and he considers that a distinct possibility. "I think I can gain more," he says. "In high school, junior college and even USC, each year was better than the last. At Buffalo, the whole future looks so bright. We're so young. The Super Bowl is the ultimate goal. At Buffalo we are dedicated to attaining that!"

Reggie McKenzie unloads on Bengal defensive tackle Ron Carpenter, enabling Dennis Shaw to throw unimpaired.

Bob Penchion stands firm ready to perform the most grueling chore in football—pass blocking.

JAMES
20

The Bills' defense lines up for the next play. Left to right they are Allen Aldridge, Jerry Patton, Dave Washington, Bob Kampa and Walt Patulski.

the new breed

jim braxton

For 45 consecutive games the Miami Dolphins had not permitted an opposing rusher to muster 100 yards. Now, nearing the end of the 1973 season, they were taking the Rich Stadium field bent on extending that streak in the face of O.J. Simpson, and clinching the AFC Eastern title as well.

The title came with a 17–0 shutout and the Dolphins held O.J. to 60 yards until the final two minutes. The Juice then came through with another 60 yards, but the Dolphin string had been broken. Fullback Jim Braxton had penetrated the Miami middle for 119 yards in 17 thrusts.

Only a few weeks earlier the Bills weren't sure the six-foot-one, 243-pound fullback would play at all in 1973. Indeed, his entire football future was clouded by a congenital lower back injury which kept him inactive for the season's first eight games. The Miami game was the proof everyone around the Bills' camp needed that Braxton could come back.

After the Miami game, Braxton was off and running, blasting into the middle of enemy defenses as the Bills dominated their final three foes and won their last four games. The Falcons, Patriots and Jets could not stand up to the Simpson-Braxton punch. Now the Bills' opposition could not concentrate just on the Juice.

Where O.J. had seen seven and even eight-man fronts in earlier games, Braxton's power kept them from playing so wide. Against Miami, when middle linebacker Nick Buoniconti would key on O.J. and hawk him wherever he went, the Juice would often be a decoy and Braxton would carry into the area vacated by Buoniconti.

Braxton finished 1973 with 494 yards and four touchdowns (including both of Buffalo's in the 17–6 upset of Atlanta) in 108 carries for a 4.6 yard average in the last six games. It was easily the most promise the big back from West Virginia had displayed since being drafted in the third round in 1971 and emerging as a starter in '72.

As a blocker, his hard cracks sprang O.J. often, and at crucial moments in the final three games. At season's end, there was no question Braxton had survived a career-menacing back injury to wrest the fullback job from Larry Watkins.

Bills' fullback Jim Braxton has increased his game yardage totals each year he has been with the team.

34
34

jim cheyunski

Jim Cheyunski (50) loses his helmet but hangs on to help bring down the Jets' John Riggins.

Linebacker Jim Cheyunski is about to make a jarring tackle.

Playing hurt is a way of life with some professional athletes and Jim Cheyunski, in his own quiet but effective way, learned firsthand in 1973 what they must endure.

Cheyunski, a principal figure in a six-player off-season trade with the New England Patriots, suffered a preseason injury that was initially considered a bad knee sprain but turned out to be a torn cartilage. The five-year veteran middle linebacker had to miss the season opener against his former team, but he returned to start the remaining 13.

Cheyunski brought stability to the linebacker corps, which in previous seasons had been a major weakness. His range was wide and his hitting rock-hard despite the painful injury.

The former Syracuse University All-American had the satisfaction of playing on a winning team for the first time in his pro career. His individual peak, however, came October 29 as the Bills were on Monday night national television for the first time and made the most of it, throttling Kansas City, 23–14, as O.J. cracked the 1,000-yard half-season barrier.

Cheyunski's staunch defensive play made way for O.J. touchdowns putting Buffalo in the lead 14–0, in the first three minutes, 37 seconds.

Quarterback Len Dawson, hawked by ends Walt Patulski and Earl Edwards, fumbled at the Kansas City 15 and "Shy" was there to recover. Moments later, O.J. scored on a one-yard burst. On the next series, Cheyunski intercepted a Dawson pass meant for Otis Taylor and weaved his way brilliantly to the four. The Juice scored from there on the next play.

As if the knee weren't enough, Jim aggravated an ankle sprain in that game and he sprained it again the following week in New Orleans. But the quality of his play remained high and the Buffalo defense stayed tough.

Linebacker Jim Cheyunski was acquired from the Patriots in a trade before the 1973 season.

"I was pleased with my play during the season," Cheyunski said, "except I had to play on the bad ankle in games like the loss in New Orleans. I really couldn't perform up to par with it. It hurt just as much against the Chiefs, but I happened to be in the right place at the right time early and made the fumble recovery and interception."

Cheyunski's remarks may be low-key, but enthusiasm in Buffalo is high. The logic is simple: If he can perform this way with an injured knee and ankle, just wait until he's healthy.

73

earl edwards

The date was September 10, 1973, the Monday before the N.F.L.'s regular season games. It also was the day marking the inter-conference trading deadline.

Bills' coach Lou Saban celebrated it by completing the deal which "made" his defensive line into a cohesive unit. He reached for six-foot-six, 265-pound Earl Edwards, who had proven his strength at defensive tackle for the tough San Francisco front four. The 49ers were willing to part with him for promising running back Randy Jackson and a 1975 third-round draft choice.

Edwards lost little time showing the techniques of a successful pass rusher. Saban moved Edwards outside to right end after the season opener and in the home opener with the New York Jets, Edwards spent most of the afternoon harassing and dropping quarterback

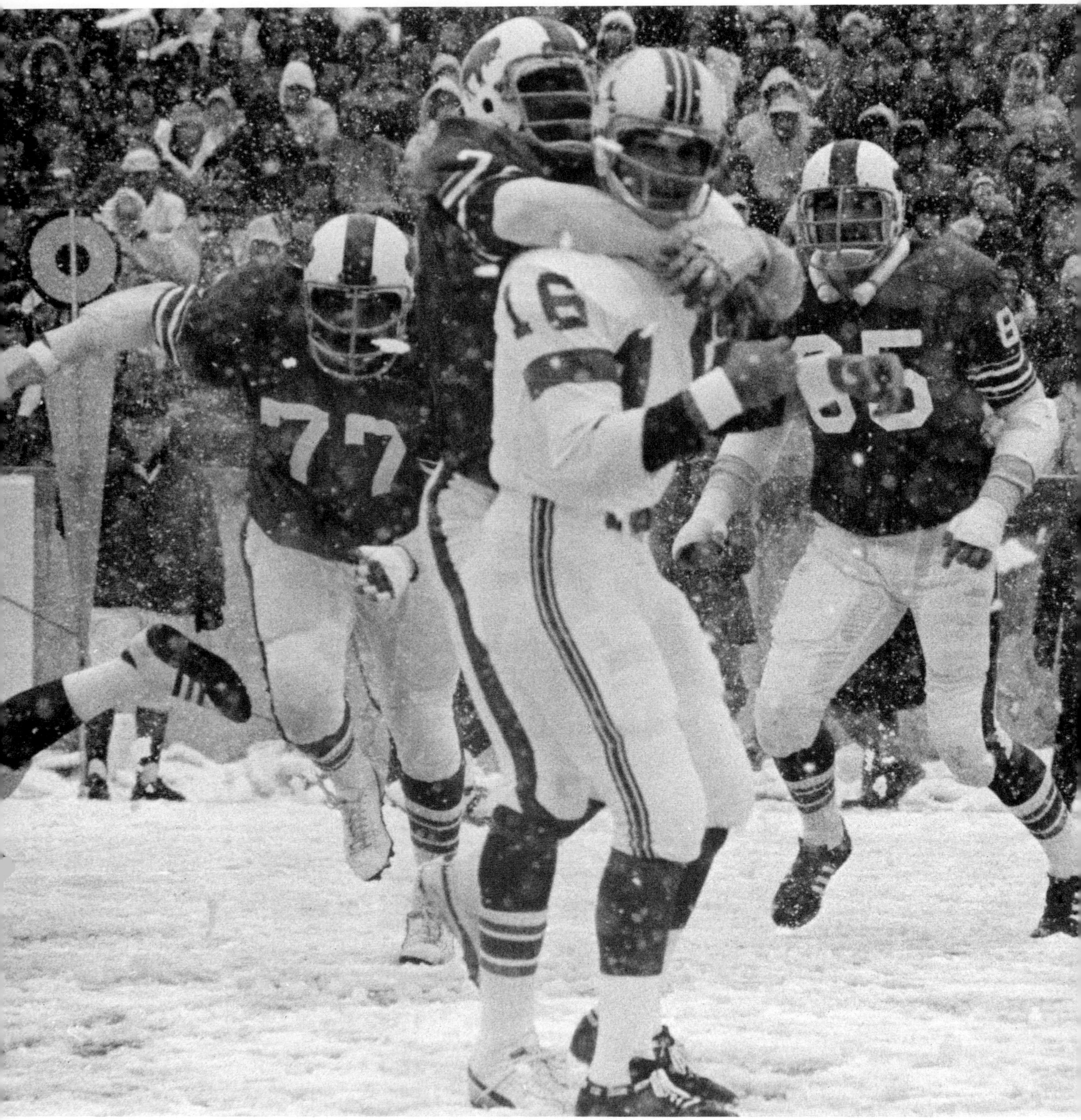

New England quarterback Jim Plunkett is collared by Earl Edwards.

Al Woodall. Tackle Bob Svihus could not contain Edwards. Robert Woods, brought in to replace the dazed Svihus could only hold Edwards and he was caught several times.

Stan Jones, the Buffalo defensive line coach who molded a powerful defensive front for Saban in Denver and is doing the same in Buffalo, said he "never saw a veteran lineman so frustrated and bewildered" as Svihus after Edwards' exhibition against the Jets.

The Bills triumphed that afternoon, 9–7, starting a three-victory homestand, a crucial step in the club's first successful season since 1966. Edwards remained solid, standing out again in the important 17–6 upset over Atlanta. After that rock-ribbed defensive showing, Earl became the "attorney" for the Buffalo defense.

"The fans and football writers have a tendency to overlook us, the guys on defense, or to take us for granted," Edwards says. "That can be discouraging. We have people on our defense who came from everywhere—from other teams, places where they played other types of defense. Now we're learning defense the Lou Saban way and we're getting there. But not many people notice."

Patulski-Patton-Kadish-Edwards constituted the united front the Bills boasted in '73 and Edwards was the leader who spurred his linemates' development. The Bills were dented for only 11 rushing touchdowns in '73 as opposed to 26 a year earlier.

joe ferguson

Can a quarterback with a disappointing senior season in college make it as a rookie starter in the National Football League?

The odds are against it but Joe Ferguson proved otherwise in 1973. He wrested the starting job from Dennis Shaw and directed Buffalo to its first winning season since 1966. The Bills were the only NFL team in 1973 to flaunt the widely accepted theory—you can't win with a rookie quarterback—and they finished 9–5.

Now, the six-foot-one, 180-pound fireball is Buffalo's top quarterback. Shaw, 1970 Rookie of the Year, became expendable and was traded to St. Louis after the season.

Coach Lou Saban has high hopes for this man—1973 rookie quarterback Joe Ferguson.

Coach Lou Saban guided Ferguson carefully and slowly, sparing him the heavy-sack treatment that has ruined many a promising quarterback. He called the plays from the bench, though Ferguson had to check off as many as one-third at the line of scrimmage. Ferguson limited the pass calls, an easy decision when O.J. Simpson is in the same backfield.

During the 11th game of the season, however, it became necessary for Ferguson to pass. Baltimore was stacking its defenses for O.J., offering seven and even eight-man fronts, daring Ferguson to throw. Losing this game would be a fourth straight defeat, and Saban had to turn him loose. Less than two minutes remained when Joe fired a tying 37-yard touchdown pass to Bob Chandler, sparking a rally that ended in a 24–17 victory.

The Bills won their remaining four games with authoritative style. Ferguson completed 11 of 19 passes for 201 yards that day in Baltimore and by the end of 1973 the Bills were no longer known as just a running team.

Ferguson realizes that without O.J., his rookie year could have been a nightmare. "He helped me in so many ways," he says. "He had such a great year, that took the pressure right away from me. Because of him, I was able to come along slowly. The linebackers, for example, had to honor his play fakes and that kept them off me."

Simpson likes the idea of Ferguson handoffs for the rest of his career. He's the quarterback of the future in Buffalo," O.J. says.

32
78

12

In the 1973 season finale Joe Ferguson hands off to burly fullback Jim Braxton . . . and again to record-shattering O.J. Simpson.

Observe: The Bills' wide receivers wear cages on their helmets.

It may seem an odd state of affairs, but it is easy to explain. With this team, headed by the NFL's premier running back, catching passes is not necessarily the primary function of a wide receiver. Blocking often is.

Some, like Haven Moses, object to blocking, insisting their game is catching passes. That's why he was traded to Denver. Others, like J.D. Hill, know their forte is the aerial game, but get warm satisfaction from a crack-back block that springs an O.J. for a long gain.

J.D. Hill, billed as the most exciting pass snatcher ever to emerge from Arizona State when the Bills made him their 1971 draft choice, never caught a touchdown pass in the Bills' revolutionary '73 campaign. The American Conference's fourth-ranking receiver, with 52 grabs for 754 yards and five touchdowns in 1972, finished 1973 with only 29 catches for 422 yards. But there are those who insist J.D.'s value increased because of his blocking exploits.

After the 34–7 loss at San Diego, in which he was a shining light with seven catches for 118 yards, J.D. was named the Bill of the Week by the *Buffalo Courier-Express.*

Many feel that J.D. is the Bills' second "name" offensive superstar despite the decrease in passing yardage. He likes to remember his first regular season game as a Bill—after he recovered from the serious knee and vertebrae injuries suffered in the first exhibition, at Detroit, that kept him out of the first 10 games of his rookie year.

"My first game back was against New England and I scored two touchdowns. I don't think I'll ever forget that day," the Bills' number one free spirit says. "We were 0–10 going into that game and it was the only game we won all year."

That was O.J. Simpson's third year of frustration in Buffalo and J.D.'s first. Individually, Hill's fortunes boomed in '72, Saban's first season of his second Buffalo tenure. His aerial production dipped as the Bills improved, thanks in no small way to his unselfish behind-the-scenes blocking exploits.

Those who observed closely realized the Bills do indeed have two superstar "initial men"—O.J. and J.D.

The Bills' 1971 number one draft choice, wide receiver J.D. Hill, paid off. He became an All-Pro in 1972.

j.d. hill

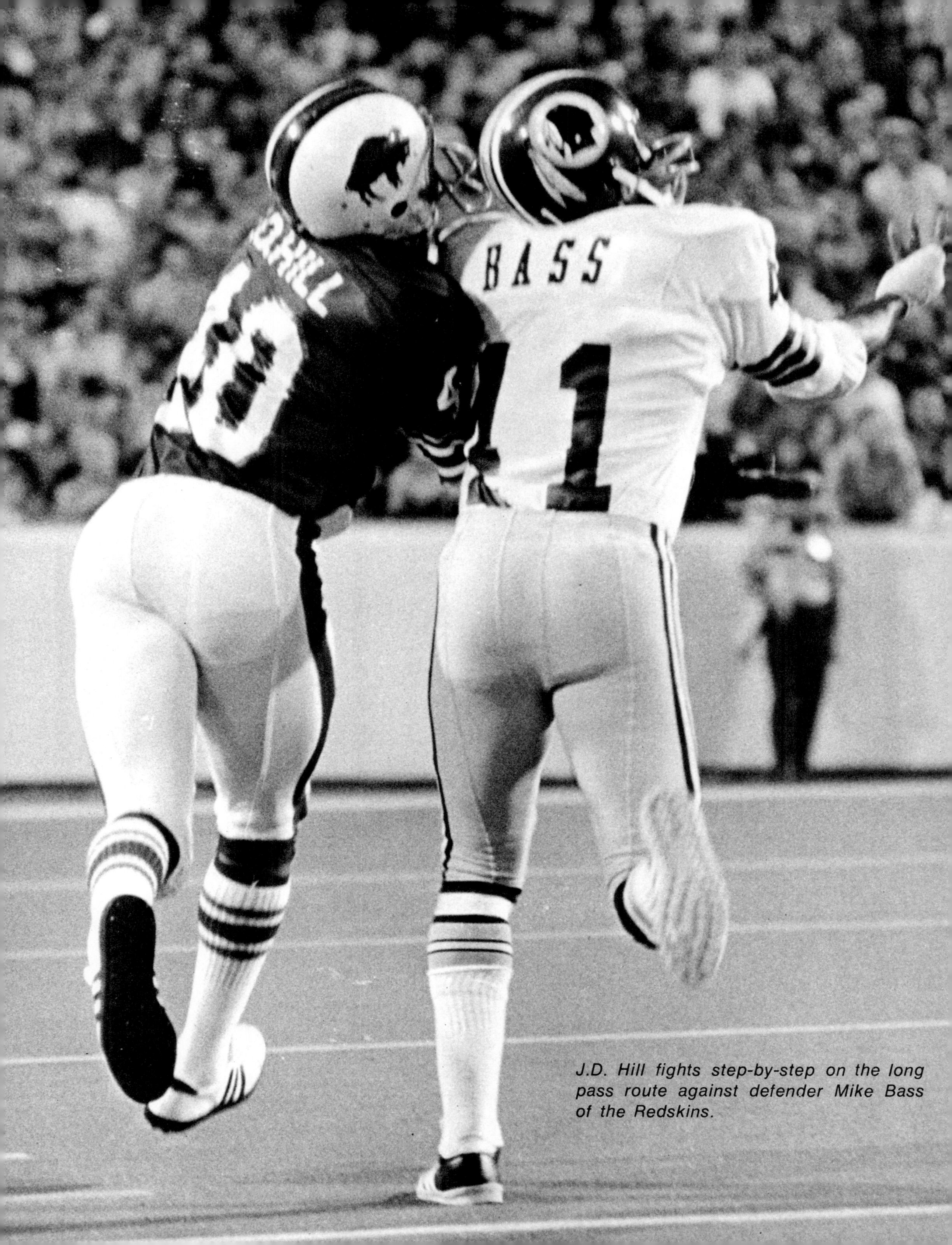

J.D. Hill fights step-by-step on the long pass route against defender Mike Bass of the Redskins.

Wide receiver J.D. Hill, one of the fastest at his position.

20

robert james

Robert James is an aggressive, tough tackler who rates as one of the best defensive backs in man-to-man coverage.

O.J. Simpson thought of the January 21, 1973 Pro Bowl as a proving ground and so did cornerback Robert James. It was James' chance to demonstrate he belonged as an All-Pro.

Oakland's tough Willie Brown occupied the other AFC corner slot that day and NFC quarterbacks Billy Kilmer and Norm Snead wanted to avoid him. They concentrated on James instead and were mighty frustrated.

In 1973, as the Bills' won-lost record soared to 9–5, James was paid the ultimate compliment. He played in pain most of the season with a bad heel bruise that left him limping during the week. Still, opposing quarterbacks stayed away from his side of the field. They would take other risks rather than tangle with James on virtually one leg. When All-Star selection time came, James was named All-Pro once again.

Cornerback Robert James tackles Marv Fleming of the Dolphins.

James, a soft-spoken gentleman who turns into a demon on the field, came up the hard way. He had played linebacker and defensive end at Fisk College and no player from that school had ever made it as a pro.

James realized he'd have to make it as a free agent. He knew his size, six-foot-one, 185 pounds, would disqualify him from the positions he'd played in college and he had no running back experience. But he possessed excellent speed and reactions, intelligence and a keen willingness to hit.

"I thought maybe I could make it as a safety or cornerback," James remembers. So did the Bills after James established himself as an eye-catching special teams performer—throwing himself through packs of bodies for chilling tackles on kickoffs and punts. He became known for his recklessness in his rookie year 1969 and, though the Bills weren't winning, the fans applauded James loudly. They loved his aggressive style.

Five years later, James and O.J. are the "graybeards" of the new, young Bills. Both suffered through four losing years to be around for the good times they deserve. Saban's housecleaning moved all around James on defense. James had long been underrated in the pro ranks, but Saban understood: it is difficult to recognize individual defensive talent if a team is consistently losing. When the housecleaning began, Saban realized the "occupied" sign was hung at one position—left corner.

20

ILLS
67
6

reggie mckenzie

In Buffalo Reggie McKenzie, the strong man from Michigan is known as O.J. Simpson's "bodyguard." He is also O.J.'s roommate, and the Juice refers to him fondly as "my main man."

The Bills' second-round draft choice behind Walt Patulski in 1972, McKenzie is rated the finest young pulling guard in the league and a consensus All-Pro.

With injuries abounding in '72, Reggie was not afforded the luxury of careful development. Instead, emergency made him an immediate starter—and he was easily the patched-up line's mainstay. In '73, with a rookie year behind him and more talented teammates flanking him, the ex-Wolverine joined the league's elite. Throughout the season, with O.J. breaking records all around him, Reggie was the team's lead blocker.

O.J. Simpson calls All-Pro guard Reggie McKenzie my "main man."

Reggie McKenzie has confidence and he plays that way. In his first two professional years he was tutored by former Green Bay great Jim Ringo, one of the best offensive linemen ever, and his quick development reflects this.

Says Coach Lou Saban: "His devotion to duty is among the finest I've ever seen. Reggie's approach to his job has been one of the major factors in our team's success and he has so many years in front of him."

After the record-smashing 1973 season finale in New York, McKenzie disclosed that he had been hoping for 2,000 yards for O.J. since training camp. "I knew he could do it all along," Reggie said. "We made sure Juice got his 2,000." When O.J. passed Brown's record, it was Reggie who checked the sideline markers and first raised his arms in triumph. He did the same when the 2,000 mark was passed.

In the dressing room, as O.J. shared the spotlight with his entire offensive unit, it was McKenzie who accepted the Washington Touchdown Club Player of the Year Award for O.J. In Buffalo, it was Reggie who presented the Dunlop Professional Athlete of the Year Award to his famous teammate. One week later, O.J. flew from his California home to New York to join in a Long Island tribute to McKenzie as "Blocker of the Year."

Reggie McKenzie up front and O.J. Simpson rushing behind with football in hand—they are a matchless combination.

67

walt patulski

Sometimes a quick trip down the ladder of fortune can be a soul-searching experience which reaps long-term benefits—as Walt Patulski learned during the 1973 season.

Patulski, an All-American star as Notre Dame's left defensive end, was the NFL's top 1972 draft choice, grabbed by the Bills as Coach Lou Saban started rebuilding the outfit in the trench positions.

The Fulton, N.Y., native seemed to make steady progress as a rookie, anchoring the left side as a starter in all 14 games. But in early '73 he found himself riding the bench for "a lack of aggressiveness," as Saban put it.

Walt Patulski was the Bills' number one draft choice in 1972, first picked in the NFL.

Patulski now had to win back the job that had been handed to him the previous year. He did, with outstanding special teams' play during a three-victory homestand, blocking several kicks and coming close numerous times. When the Bills took a 4–1 record to Miami, Patulski was in the starting lineup again. Determined not to relinquish the post again, he became a weekly terror to Bills' opponents.

"My entire frame of mind changed when I was benched," Patulski says. "When I was demoted, I realized I could wind up out in the street like anyone else. It changed my whole life and my approach to it."

Patulski proved his mettle that year in Baltimore where he was instrumental in starting the season-climaxing four-game victory run. Patulski deflected three passes, made five tackles including a sack of quarterback Marty Domres, and assisted on two other stops against the Colts, earning him Associated Press Defensive Player of the Week honors. The six-foot-six, 260-pound titan was smiling broadly now. The "dark" month on the bench was behind him. Football was fun again.

Saban laughs at the "lack of aggressiveness" tag now. "Walt's future is excellent," he says. "Once he came back, he just kept playing better all the time. Once a big man learns the techniques, he just keeps going uphill."

One segment of Bills' fans regularly hangs a banner at Rich Stadium now. It reads, "The Pole Patrol to the Super Bowl," and refers chiefly to Walt Patulski.

85

70

Walt Patulski leaps to block a Sonny Jurgensen pass, while Bob Kampa (70) applies additional pressure.

Seldom has a professional football team enjoyed as successful a collegiate draft as did the Bills in 1973, with 10 of the 21 players selected making the final roster and four emerging as immediate starters.

Tight end Paul Seymour and guard Joe DeLamielleure joined quarterback Joe Ferguson to inject new life into the offense. When the defense took the field there was rookie linebacker John Skorupan.

When it comes to linebacking, pro scouts look first to Penn State—with good reason. Among the 17 Penn State products playing in the NFL in 1973 seven were backers. Skorupan is Buffalo's golden Penn Stater.

After impressing in the Chicago All-Star Game against Miami, Skorupan stepped in at the Bills' strong side post and was an immediate hit. Linebacking had been the Bills' "Achilles heel" in previous seasons but John's hard-hitting, heady play quickly brightened the picture.

In late season, when many Bills' followers were touting Ferguson as the club's top Rookie of the Year candidate, veteran middle linebacker Jim Cheyunski disagreed. "Skorupan should get it if anyone does," the ex-Patriot said. "You just don't see rookies step in and do the job the way he has."

Coach Lou Saban paid Skorupan a low-key tribute after the season and a bigger one in the 1974 draft. "As a first-year man, John did an excellent job," Saban said. "He improved with every game and has a very bright future." The draft brought the real stamp of approval when in the second round, Saban went back to the same source, Penn State, and tabbed Doug Allen as a linebacker, to be reunited with Skorupan on the '74 Bills.

Entering pro ball, the "rap" on Skorupan was he would not have the speed to be consistently effective and that is probably what kept Skorupan from being drafted earlier than the sixth round. But he had no running problem at all, and in addition his tremendous instinct for the ball—exceptionally developed for a rookie—enabled him to throw enemy runners for losses on a good number of occasions.

During the season, as the Bills' defense received many standing ovations from their Rich Stadium supporters, a steady Skorupan was usually a principal reason.

John Skorupan (55) makes Patriot John Tarver run wide of the line of scrimmage.

john skorupan

J.D.HILL
40
SIMPSON
32